Geoengineering Poetry and Colour Photos, Vol 2!

Biography:

David was inducted as an International Poet of Merit with the International Society of Poetry in America in 1997 and made it to the semi-finals of a poetry competition there between 2000 selected poets from all over the world. He has had poetry published in South African and International magazines and newspapers and was listed in the International Who's Who of Poetry in 2012. He has released quite a number of poetry books, lots with matching photographs, also POKE POetic joKE books and Tattoo/Body Art books. He has also released CDs with poetry and music. All CDs to date recorded and produced in South Africa. Please check out his website with links to the books and CDs on www.davidnicoll.co.uk The CDs are also on YouTube and Spotify!

There have been lyric videos made from some select tracks which are also on the website as well as a performance videos by others section which is great performances by fellow Poets and Musicians in the days BC!*

*=Before Corona!

All my videos are now removed as YouTube have closed my channel after banning two previous online book launches.they dont want anyone speaking the truth about what is really going on.

The poems in this book have been taken from my previuos series of books,

Scottish Thoughts and Reflections Vols 1-10.

Please join us if you care about this beautiful home of ours.

This book released on the 11th August 2021

Printed via Amazon.co.uk

First Printing, 11th August 2021

ISBN 9798453769117

www.davidnicoll.co.uk

david@davidnicoll.co.uk

We care about the planet and all life forms on it, we also object to many planes leaving long white streaks all over our skies and blocking out our sunshine amongst other things. Please join us if you do as well.

Face book groups:

SMAAPP Scottish Musicians and Artistes Against the Poisoning of our Planet

And

Anti Geoengineering Scotland.

Thank you to my Anti Geoengineerng friends for the use of some of your photographs

With the poetry!

Including Kim Arnold, Emory Eugene Mullen, Momo Clark,

Previous publications:

CDs all on YouTube and Spotify:

David Nicoll and friends Vols 1,2 and 3

With great thanks to the many friends and musicians who contributed

To the making of these CDs through my years in South Africa.

In collaboration with

Great thanks to Mervyn Fuller and friends for his musical creations.

Created in Gaansbai, Cape Town, South Africa.

I was the lyricist in the band known as MAD,

**Mervyn and Myself became freinds a number of years ago, he was a retired singer
Songwriter who used to play the music circuits in South Africa.**

We lived a long way apart and every now and again he would phone me and say,

Write something about this! Then he would give me an idea which would spark me,

Would then write down the lyrics and send them to him. He would then decide

What type of song to make it, Rock, Reggae, Easy listening? Then put it together

And pull his friends Mike Pregnolatu to add lead Guitar and Mike Laatz on Saxophone.

The idea behind the MAD CDs is for you to listen to tracks

Where you resonate with the track titles.

Mervyn And Dave:

CDs

Treat it so!

This is MAD 2!

On Days like These!

The Best of MAD!

The Beat goes on!

On the Home Straight!

Index:

It is all about Control!

It Out!

Let it be!

Liberty Away!

Manifest!*

More!*

Not See!*

Of Humanity!

One!*

Our Skies

Party!

Philanthropy!

Poisonous Spray!*

Prevail!

Regret!

Save!

Silver grey!

So High!*

Spray!*

Spraying!*

Stealing Our sunshine!*

Sun away!*

Sunshine Away!*

The Only Way

The Smokescreen!

Their Lies!

Tranquility!

Today!*

Us Out!

We do Not Consent!*

What are These Long White Streaks in The sky?

Whilst You Can!*

Wolf!*

Your Face!*

EMFs Electro Magnetic Frequency charts.

The way clouds used to be.

New cloud formations.

Common types of clouds.

Standard Cloud type chart.

Geoengineering Photo Gallery.

Again!

Seeing

This

Sign

Might

Cause

Some

Strain,

Looks

Like,

The

Scottish

Ruling

Parties,

Ariel

Branch,

Strike

Again!

Any way!

New laws,

Now imposed

On the

Majority!

Of

Global,

Humanity!

Where we,

Are no

Longer free!

Where now,

Is

Democracy?

Seems that we,

Are moving,

More

Into

Communism,

To me!

With a halt

To all

Gatherings,

Socialising,

Church,

Work

And

Pub going,

Living in a

Mask wearing,

Society!

Sitting in

Home

Imprisonment!

For over

Twelve months now,

Not at all

Funny!

All across

The world,

In almost

Every nation,

Economies,

Collapsing,

To be followed,

Shortly thereafter,

By mass

Starvation!

Increasing stress

And frustration!

MSM lies,

Geoengineered

Skies,

60GHz mm

Microwaves

Leaving you

Short of breath,

In heaves or sighs?

Giving

Our strength away,

To politicians,

Who,

In others

Pockets,

They stay!

Whose

Hidden agendas,

They promote

And from them,

Fear to stray!

Now promoting

Mandatory

Vaxxinations!

To take your

Freedom away!

We must

Rise up together

And say!

"We

Do not

Consent,

To any,

Of this,

Crap!

In

Any Way!"

COVID-19 SHEEP

To demonstrate my obedience to the government, I will willingly imprison myself. I will follow ever increasing restrictions because the government is much smarter than I. I will sit and obey every command because they are just trying to save me from my bad decisions.

I hereby surrender all my rights. I have demonstrated that I don't understand or deserve them.

_____   _____
Gavin Newsom, Supreme Protector   Sheep Signature   Date

You don't need to keep this in your wallet. You will be sitting at home when the government comes to call on you

As they Spray!

Isn't it a Miracle Wull Boyle? All these Rare Sun Dogs showing up all over the place, on the same day and getting blamed by the weather man on Ice Crystals! Even though in the morning, we have photos of the planes as they spray!

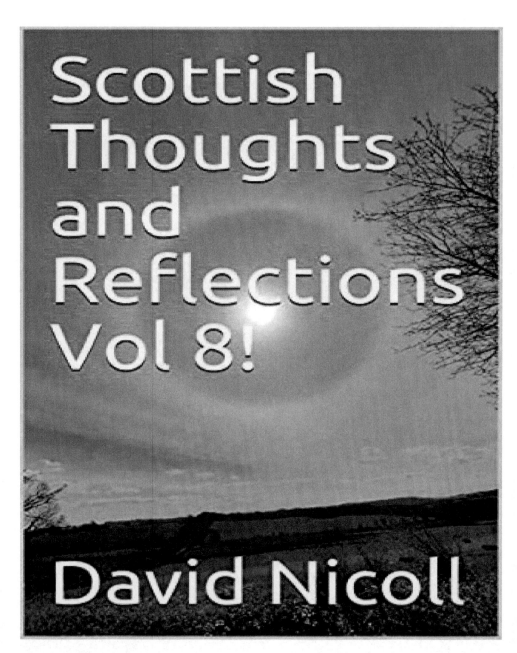

Scottish
Thoughts
and
Reflections
Vol 8!

David Nicoll

Photo by Momo Clark!

Bard!

Finding
A job now,
Is really hard!
So please,
Cash in
Some of your
Cryptocurrency,
Buy the book
And
Support,
Your
Local
Bard!

Bill (God) Gates!

He's

Funding

The

Spraying,

Of

Toxic

Particles,

In the

Global air!

Leaving

Many,

With

Dementia,

Altzheimers

And

Many

Another,

Serious

Issue,

Needing

Medical care!

Geoengineering,

They call it,

To block,

Out

The Sun,

They

Spray,

Then the

Nexrads,

Dopplers

And

HAARPs,

Are

Turned on,

Creating lines,

In the Spray!

Which then,

Spread out

And

Hide,

The

Sun,

Away!

All

Over,

Silver

Grey!

Sometimes,

This can last,

For many

A day!

Stops your

Vegetables,

From

Growing

So well,

Fruit trees

Reportedly,

Not doing

Very well!

Reduced

Sunlight,

Is not good

For any

Life forms,

No matter

What

Anyone,

Does say!

But he

Makes

Choices,

Over us,

On manys

A day!

Billionaires

Mainly,

Some are mates,

With

Our

New

World

Leader

Mr Bill (God) Gates!

and that was the day that
Bill Gates decided to
murder all of humanity

Buzzing!

Was just saying

To a friend in Glasgow,

While talking about,

The switching on

Next month of Five Gee!

That it should be,

A very interesting time,

As far as I can see!

What with

All the spraying,

Going on

From planes above,

With Nano Particles,

Of Aluminium,

Barium and Strontium,

They are certainly not

Put there in love!

They will now

Be in our bloodstream

And also our brain!

This is sure to create

Some strain!

We may well

Never recover?

Or be healthy

Again?

He plays

For a band,

Likes to hit

The djembe drum

And sing!

Said to him that

This time

Next month,

We could be

Buzzing!

Glaswegian sky from my back garden!

Calamity!

Hi from Scotland, the land that used to be known as, Of the Brave and Free! But there is not, nowadays, too much, of either, Commodity! As the Majority, take their daily fear and instructions from the TV! Which makes them blind to see, the unfolding Calamity!

Cloud!

A

Chemical

Concoction!

Although

Not

Said,

Aloud!

This

Is,

A

Blanket,

Of

Artificial Cloud!

CONtrail!

What on earth

Do we have to do?

To get the world to see?

That these long white

Streaks spreading

Across the sky,

Are not put there

Innocently!

They are not put there

For no reason,

They are not put there

For fun!

One of the reasons is

To block out the Sun!

This they do

Most definitely!

As the Sun

Gets hidden behind

A hazy screen,

As all can see!

They are sprayed

Across almost

Every nation!

Coal fly ash and

Other things

Is what they are,

Taken for free,

From many

A power station!

They contain,

Nano particles

Which when breathed in

Can lodge in your brain!

The very fact,

That this is being done

Is absolutely,

Insane!

Barium, Strontium

And Aluminium too!

Affects all living

Lifeforms on this planet,

As we daily pass through!

What can you do?

Well please think about it,

That would be a start!

Wonder how your children

And grandchildren's

Future will be,

When you are apart!

This is done

With malice

And not with love!

For if it is

Not allowed,

To go up a

Power stations

Chimney stacks,

Then why should

It be sprayed above?

Dementia and

Alzheimer's deaths

Now going off the scale,

Bees, insect's, plants, trees,

Also dying off!

This spraying is creating

Global DIS -EASE!

Weather manipulation,

Is also part of the game,

Without a doubt,

Creating Cyclones,

Snowstorms, Hurricanes,

Floods and drought!

It is almost enough

To make you wail!

When you ask someone

"What is that?"

And they reply

"A CONtrail!"

Photo by Kim Arnold!

CONtrail!

Nowadays,

We have

Information

And

Disinformation,

Truth,

Or

Lies?

Planes,

Spreading

Long white streaks,

In our skies!

This story,

Works

For the masses,

It's rarely,

That it does

Fail!

As the

Propaganda

In the

Main Stream Media,

Have hypnotised

Them into

Believing,

That,

It is,

A

CONtrail!

Covertly!

Some subjects,

That are

Avoided by the

New movement,

Known as XR!

Started from nowhere,

Now globally,

A rising star!

They make no mention

Of Geoengineering,

EMFs, Electro Magnetic

Frequencies or Five Gee?

Even although,

These long white

Streaks in the sky,

Are there,

For

Everyone to see!

They are in almost

Every nation,

Another thing,

That they don't discuss,

Is weather manipulation!

Why is this now?

Why should this be?

Unless

Maybe?

Behind the scenes,

The organisers,

They are

Involved,

Covertly?

COMET458
Royal Air Force (RAF)

© Ian Howat

BZZ
BRIZE NORTON
Departed 01:05 ago

N/A

CALIBRATED ALT.
4,153 ft
GROUND SPEED
236 kts

Airbus A400M

REG: ZM405

3D view · Route · More info · Follow · Share

Cutting Edge!

This was the plane!

D Away!

Yet another,

Contrived,

Glaswegian

Grey day!

To keep,

The

Sunshine

And

Vitamin D

Away!

Dis-Ease!

Just saw a

New thing today!

Two planes flying

An identical course,

One slightly

In front and higher

Than the other,

With both,

Releasing long white

Dissipating spray!

From the ground it would

Appear that

There is only one trail!

But they will be intermingling

Into one as one the winds

These Nano particulates sail!

Why does nobody

See these things?

Or even wonder why?

Planes leaving

Long white spreading streaks,

All over our sky!

This observation made

In the Isle of Mull,

In the Inner Hebrides!

At peace with nature,

Mind and body at ease!

While these b#stards

In the sky spray ultimate

Death and

Dis-Ease!

Enough!

Tweet by Nicola Sturgeon 0n 08.07.2019

"Scottish summer sunset,

Love the light at this time of year!"

"Love the light

At this time of year!"

The trails in

Front of the Sun

Will bring everyone's

Demise closer

And will not

Bring them

Any good cheer!

Are they

Natural cloud forms

Or were they

Birthed by a plane?

Increasing dementia

And Alzheimer's

As the Aluminium

Nano particles

Inside them,

Once inhaled,

Coagulate and lodge

In your brain!

But being at the top,

Must be really tough

So, let's just agree!

"Aye, it's a fine Sunset

Right Enough!"

Every Single Day!

Momo Clark its election time again in Scotland as we can see! With the roll out of the Ariel branch, of the ruling party! No time now, to sit on the fence, as God, gives us signs of our Imminent Independence! At least that, is what some, die hard supporters, do say! But we know that, in fact, these streaks, were birthed by aircraft, which in our skies, they Spray! A new political party, has been formed now! The Freedom Alliance, it is opposed to Lock Down, where they makes prisoners of us, in our own homes, every single day!

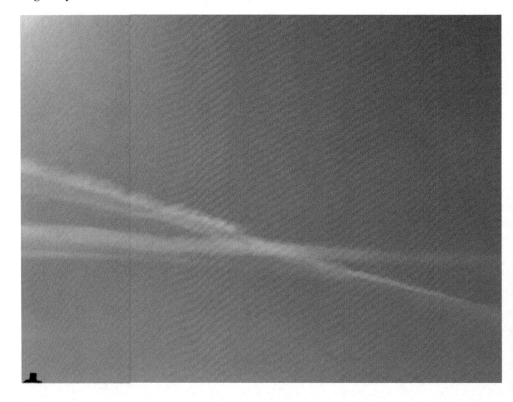

F All!

Geez that is a wild pic Momo Clark we sure got hit that day, eh! I wonder how many people actually thought about it? Apart from asking for submissions on beautiful sunsets, I came across yesterday, "Ooh isn't that beautiful!" Is what they say! I showed a mate before, that is also, what he did say! Sometimes you say, Oh woe is me! What is wrong with the Majority? That they just cannot see? Is it Brainwashing by the MSM and TV? Could be? Not on FlightRadar, so they fly untracked, with complete Authority and Impunity! Otherwise, these planes, could not just use, our Airspace, so easily! This is a really crazy call! If you think that the main problem we have is the Flu! Then you dont know F All!

Forgiven!

Like a

Stairway,

To

Heaven,

In

A

Strange,

Kind,

Of

Way,

With

The

Rungs,

Going,

Up

And

Away!

They

Came,

From

Planes,

That

Flew

By!

And

Left

Them,

In the

Sky!

They

Were

Not even,

Flying,

Very high!

You

Can see,

How it

Spreads,

Slowly!

To

Block

Out

The

Sun,

Pretty

Quickly!

While

People,

On the

Ground,

Dont even

Notice them,

Certainly not,

The

Majority!

They never

Look up,

No interest,

Controlled,

By the

Telly,

The

BBC!

All

News

And

Statistics,

Things to keep,

In your

Head!

While at night,

You

Silently

Dread,

Without

Ever

Noticing,

What is

Going on,

Outside,

Right over,

Your

Own head!

We are being

Geoengineered!

They just

Never said!

No ones

Consent,

Was ever asked,

And none

Was

Given!

Will

They,

For what,

They are

Doing,

Ever

Be

Forgiven?

Frogs!

Strange things

Are happening nowadays!

You know the score!

Now everyone,

Is in Lock Down!

Are these the days?

Like George Orwell says,

In his book called 1984?

We have SMART TVs

That watch us,

Phones that listen

And say where you are!

Alexa's and Echo's,

That listen intently,

To your every word

 And answer,

To your every desire!

 A Fridge that can order milk,

No one allowed

To visit theatres, restaurants,

Clubs or bars,

No visiting anyone,

Two metre exclusion zones

And soon

Driverless cars!

Draconian laws enacted

With massive fines,

Or even jail?

For being out,

Without a

Reasonable excuse,

Who decides that?

Protesting would

Have very little,

Impact on that!

Not allowed,

Even to visit

Your own family!

Grandparents,

Grandchildren,

Brothers, sisters,

Fathers, mothers,

Each other,

Wanting and longing,

To see!

With everywhere shut,

And no free

Movement allowed,

Seems kind of scary!

And all of this

Is because of a modified

Flu Virus known as

C_V_D!

Which doesn't kill

As many as they would

Have you believe,

But just about everyone

Who has died recently,

Gets listed as

Dying

WITH

It,

Not

FROM it!

You see?

The figures looking

And sounding like a

Real urgency!

An Emergency!

The main stream media

And TV,

Keeping a focus

On it,

Statistically!

A common denominator

Is maintaining fear,

In all publications,

TheInternet,

The

Hypnotic and

Multi

"PROGRAMMED"

And Programming,

TV!

Families without incomes,

Can't work,

Run out of food!

All over the world,

Many hardships,

From this

Inflated Pandemic,

This is everywhere,

In every land!

Europe, America,

China, Spain, South Africa,

Australia and

New Zealand!

Censorship and

Monitoring of every

Individual is ongoing!

Few with many reasons,

In this situation,

Of self imprisonment,

And global

House arrest,

With the heart

To sing!

Planes leaving long white

And black sprays in the skies,

With very few humans

Thinking,

What are they?

Although they see

Them every day,

With their own eyes!

The Sun being blocked

Behind a silvery haze!

With watery eyes,

At the

Artificial cloud

You gaze!

Unreal sunsets and sunrises

The colours too bright,

Getting sprayed

From above in both day

And night!

60GHz mm Microwaves,

The new invisible,

Technology!

Beaming out

From millions of masts!

Many things do they see!

And are actually

A weapon,

Used by

The military!

This causes the molecules

Of Oxygen to spin!

Creating problems,

With transferring to

Our Haemoglobin,

Leaving a shortness of breath,

Dry cough

And ultimately,

Death!

Exact same symptoms

As this new Flu!

But if you die

It will be listed,

As that because

The doctors,

Have been told,

That this is what

They have to do!

Hospitals asking older patients,

Dementia and Autism

Sufferers outside too,

To sign DNR forms,

Which is

"Do

Not

Resuscitate!"

Unbelievable

But true!

So how do we?

Get ourselves out

Of our self imposed jail?

Should we protest?

Mmmm can't do that now?

It would lead to massive fines

That you don't need,

Not here nor in any nation!

A fine is the best case scenario,

The other is

They give you,

Unlimited term of

Free accommodation!

This all without even

A court case,

Is this not

Subjucation?

The only way out,

That our new

God called Bill sees,

Is in his glasses screens!

The only way out,

Is for the whole worlds

Population to get

Injected with Vaxxines!

But this will take time,

No mass gatherings allowed,

He protested!

What he didn't say was that

They will also be untested!

It seems now

That many of our freedoms,

They did strip!

Word says

That it will include,

An RFID chip!

Ruled by a global

Banking elite!

Who have things

Pretty well tied up,

For them it is sweet!

Depopulation is required,

Their chosen number

Of half a billion,

People on the planet,

Is cast in stone,

On one Georgia

Guidestone!

Devil worship,

Kids for sex

And Sacrifice!

Not good at all

Can in no way

Be described as nice!

A thought here

As this rocky road

That we nowadays ride,

We are for nature,

So the creator!

Must be

On our side!

Many billions of people

Of these subjects,

They are unaware!

As into their

Cell phones,

They hypnotically stare!

What way to freedom?

Once again,

We do not understand?

We are like

Sitting in a big pot,

Treated like dogs,

As the water

Boils around The Frogs!

Game!

Just a very small

Percentage of people

In this beautiful Scottish land,

Have gathered together

As

Anti Geoengineering Scotland!

To awaken all the others

To threats,

That they neither see,

Nor understand!

But they are aware

Of the threat

From the sky,

Showing itself

As many

Long white spreading streaks,

Which cover our Sun

And sky!

Spread by anonymous planes,

But with government consent

That much we know!

As if it wasn't agreed to,

Then these planes,

From the skies

Our Air Force would blow!

Why do so few know?

Are you getting sick?

Are you feeling weak?

The doctor's attention,

For one unknown reason

Or another?

Do you need to seek?

Do you have a buzzing

In your head?

Even while

Lying in bed?

Or is there someone

That you know,

That to hospital must go?

Suffering from Dementia

Or Alzheimers,

Creating in their families

Lots of grief and pain!

Both ultimately caused,

By a coagulation

Of Aluminium

Nano particles,

In your brain!

How did this happen?

You might well sigh,

Well the reason

Is because these particles,

Came from the sky!

Many, many families now

Affected, never again

To be the same!

As we are all just

Pawns in the

Illuminati`s

Game!

Anti GeoEngineering Scotland
GeoEngineering is a crime against humanity
Every day there is an assault on Scotlands skies.
Find us on Facebook
Anti GeoEngineering Scotland
Photographs taken in South Lanarkshire.

SCOTLANDS SKIES
ARE UNDER ATTACK

Geoengineering!

The majority of people

On this beautiful planet,

All with their own lifestyles,

Culture, religion,

History and tales!

When they see these,

Long white streaks,

In the sky,

They think

Nothing of them

And call them

CONtrails!

Busy with their lives,

Busy in their actions!

Minds being taken over,

By one or another

Modern day,

Distractions!

Never thinking

Of what is going on

Above their head!

Both during the daytime

And when

Lying in bed!

Up to no good,

These planes spread

Nano particles,

Of Aluminium,

And other

Nasty things,

There will be

Barium and

Strontium,

Which are not good,

For either you,

Or your brood!

They call it

Geoengineering!

Does that

Make a bell ring?

They are not

Doing this for fun!

One of their aims

Is to block out

The Sun!

This it does

Most successfully!

As after a

Couple of hours,

After spraying,

The Sun,

You cannot see!

Which leaves mankind

Lacking in

Intake of,

Vitamin D!

Consisting of

Coal fly ash

Hell to pay,

When the dawning

Of this knowledge

In Humanity

Rings!

Although

When it will happen?

We have not got a date,

But if it is not soon,

That everyone

Wakes up,

Then I have a feeling

That it might be

Too late!

Some things

That these sprays

Can do to you!

Look out for

These symptoms,

In your family,

Friends,

Or even in you?

For they are true!

It will make people sick,

That is for sure!

These are some of

The things

That affect people,

From Nano particle

Exposure!

This will disturb them,

They will not be at ease!

With Neurological,

Parkinson's,

Or Alzheimer's

Disease?

Dementia is another

That is what they say!

Why is it now,

The number one killer

Of women in the UK?

Bronchitis, Asthma,

Emphysema

And Cancer too!

When you

Breathe it in,

There is little

That you can do!

Heart disease,

Dermatitis,

Kidney and liver

Disease!

Will leave you

Bed ridden

And not feeling

At ease!

So wake up,

Shake up!

And lift your head high!

Look at what is happening

Above your heads,

In your sky!

We are all

In this together,

There is no

Plan (et) B!

We must save

The future for our children

And our Mother Earth!

As there is nothing

That could be

Of more worth!

So next time

For your education,

While in your

Computer screen

Or cell phone?

You are peering!

Please,

Google

Geoengineering!

Chemtrail Geo-engineering

DISEASES ASSOCIATED TO NANOPARTICLE EXPOSURE

C. Buzea, I. Pacheco, & K. Robbie, *Nanomaterials and nanoparticles: Sources and toxicity, Biointerphases 2 (2007) MR17-MR71*

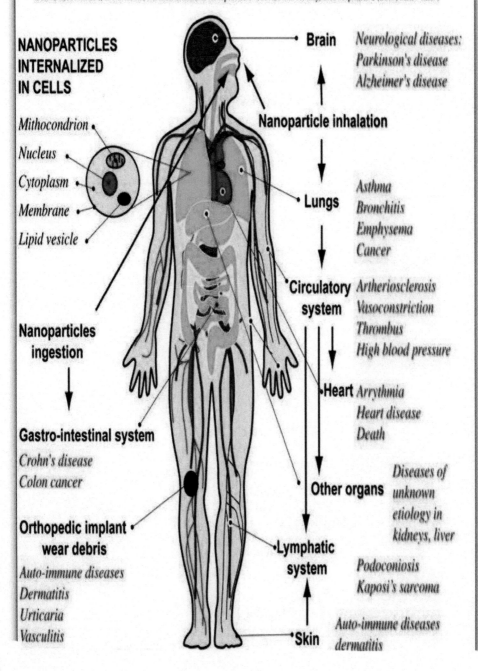

NANOPARTICLES INTERNALIZED IN CELLS

Mithocondrion
Nucleus
Cytoplasm
Membrane
Lipid vesicle

Nanoparticles ingestion

Gastro-intestinal system
Crohn's disease
Colon cancer

Orthopedic implant wear debris
Auto-immune diseases
Dermatitis
Urticaria
Vasculitis

Brain
Neurological diseases:
Parkinson's disease
Alzheimer's disease

Nanoparticle inhalation

Lungs
Asthma
Bronchitis
Emphysema
Cancer

Circulatory system
Artheriosclerosis
Vasoconstriction
Thrombus
High blood pressure

Heart
Arrythmia
Heart disease
Death

Other organs
Diseases of unknown etiology in kidneys, liver

Lymphatic system
Podoconiosis
Kaposi's sarcoma

Skin
Auto-immune diseases
dermatitis

Glasgow!

These long

White streaks

In the sky!

About

Which

Very few,

Care

To know!

Are

Sprayed

There,

Geoengineering,

Solar

Radiation

Management

And

Strategic

Aerosol

Injection

They are

Called,

Good

Morning

From

Glasgow!

Go Away!

Day after day,

They spray!

Its time,

For

Them,

To

Go Away!

Ground!

What an interesting situation

We live in today!

With many unknown aircraft,

In the skies above our heads,

Toxic chemicals they spray!

Chemtrails are called

A conspiracy!

Although they criss cross

Our skies for all

With eyes to see!

There are none so blind,

As those who cannot see!

Then there is the situation

With the roll out of Five Gee!

With microwaves

Filling the air!

Sure to leave lots

With illness

And in despair!

So we are being poisoned

From above

Sent with malice,

Certainly not love!

A massive increase

In respiratory disease

Alzheimers, Parkinsons,

ADHD, Downs Syndrome

And Dementia,

Creating in many

Global families,

Extreme Dis-Ease!

Changing times here,

At least that is what

I have found!

Poisons

In the

Sky

And

Microwaves,

On the ground!

High!

Strange rings

In the sky!

Wisping on by!

Are they

Natural?

Or,

Did they

Come,

From

A

Spout,

On

A

Plane?

Flying

Way

Up

High!

I Mean!

We do have a

Buzz in Scotland

From

Time to time,

Even though

We are in,

Lock Down,

Such a crazy,

Scene!

 If

You

Know,

What

I mean?

It is all about Control!

There is one thing

That really gets to me,

The logic in it,

I just cannot see?

For the

Special attention,

That it gets,

But

ONLY IN,

Scotland,

Are they

Banned you see!

Now how can this be?

Bagpipes the

Fighting Heart,

Spirit and Life,

In our History!

Many times

Have they been

At the front,

With soldiers

In battle!

Injured

Or dead?

Frequently!

Now we live our lives,

Silently!

Self imprisoned,

In our own cells,

Watching the TV!

Drawing

UIF,

Pension or

Furlough Money?

Getting the new

Rules, Regulations,

And Statistics daily!

Politically represented,

By our,

Commander in Cheif

Latest conditions on our

Measures put in place,

For our

Health and Safety!

Also,

How our pockets could be?

Attacked,

Ferociously by

Enormous fines imposed,

Where no one got hurt!

Nothing was stolen!

There was no victim!

Merely a

Legality!

Imposed under

Admiralty Law,

The Law of the Sea!

Not Common or

Universal law,

Due to

Imposed restrictions,

Due to a supposed,

Pandemic

Emergency!

Which has basically

Taken away,

Our

Freedom and Liberty!

Deliberately destroyed,

Our Economy!

And the majority

Are scared shitless,

Of something

That they cannot,

Even see!

Living in fear!

No good cheer!

Dreaming of days

Gone by of memory!

When we were free!

Now only History,

Looks like these days

Are now in our History!

But still the Majority,

Even this truth they do not see!

Ignorance may be bliss,

But you might find

Some pause for thought

And things are getting

Dangerous now and deadly!

The world moving in the direction,

Of Agenda 2021 and 30!

Skin peircing and injection,

With Chemical Concoctions,

Including dubious ingredients

Seems to be fashionable lately!

Have heard that it could even be,

One dayMandatory?

With Vaxxine passports

Already in place in Israel

And an upcoming ID 2020!

With Bill (God) Gates

Name and image popping up

Very frequently!

Telling us,

What is happening

And what

He,

Would like to be!

Is this the

New

Leader of the World?

Well,

Apparently!

As he flails his hands round,

Very frequently!

Funding Geoengineering,

Spraying our global skies!

With toxic chemicals,

Spread in trails,

Then blocking the Sun!

So that it,

We don't see!

Funding Monsanto and GMO!

Funding the seven main

Vaxxine makers!

Buying up farms

After terrible floods,

In the

American Mid Country!

But the weather

Gets manipulated,

For him,

Fortunately!

Possibly even

Arranged beforehand?

As they were

Bought after the events,

Relatively,

Cheaply!

Stop eating cows,

Eat his Synthetic meat,

Another

Emperors dream!

With Elon's Electric cars,

And sattelite launching,

Another step in the scheme!

To introduce us all to the

Spiritually free,

Dystopic existence

With

Artificial intellegence,

Inside nano forms,

Working silently!

Communicating and locating

In the IOT!

Working along with the hastily,

Installed during the Lock Down

60GHz mm Microwave technology!

Beaming out its invisible,

But tangible high and low,

Electro Magnetic Frequency!

Can be picked up on

EMF meters easily!

Most definately!

Affecting your own,

Electro magnetic body,

It can all be,

Altered by changes

In its Frequency!

60 GHz is the

Oxegen molecules

Spinning frequency!

Which could lead to

An apparent shortage

Of it inside your body!

Which is no doubt why,

The people in

Wuhan collapsed

In the street,

Suddenly and

Shockingly!

Wuhan had just

Switched it on,

A month previously!

Just before

The virus outbreak,

Coincidemtally!

So what might

Appear to be?

Flu symptoms,

Might not necessarily be?

It stops the transfer

Of Oxegen to the

Heamoglobin in the blood,

Depriving the brain

And organs internally,

But now it is taboo,

To speak of such things as

They are part of the plan,

For many a

Smart city!

Others like me,

Suffer from a

High pitch ringing

In the ears,

Constantly!

Only changing at times,

In Pitch,

Volume or Frequency?

With more than one

Service Provider in each city!

Different outcomes,

Or variables inevitably!

Now with satellites

Also beaming,

Reflecting and magnifying

This new technology!

That nowhere on the planet,

Could you be and not be found,

Tracked and Traced,

With everywhere coverage

Of Five and now Six Gee!

Technology!

In the meantime we,

Sit under house arrest,

Uncomfortably!

And

Unendingly!

For the sound

And feel of Bagpipes

Once more,

We wait longingly!

And notice the similarity,

How the English once before

Banned them and the tartans,

In 1746, part of our history!

The difference is,

That this law was

Imposed by our own,

National party!

It is laughable really!

Because in reality,

Across the border,

You could play away,

Quite merrily!

Taking away our Spirit,

Taking away our Soul!

What this tells me,

Is that It is nothing

To do with a Virus,

It is all about Control!

It Out!

Strange things
Happening,
In our
Skies today!
As almost
Every day,
They Spray!
Leaves us with
Different situations
That we can see!
Like hailstones,
That are
Not hard,
But feel,
Spongy!
Or Snow,
That when put
In a Microwave
Will flash
And short it out,
Because it contains
Metallic,
Nano
Particulates,
Without a doubt!
Next time,
That it
Snows,
In your area,
Please try,
It out!

Let it be!

Hi Robert

They get really pissed off, with what we both say, eh! Without a doubt, because the one thing that they dont want, is to, let the Truth out! But right is right and wrong is wrong! The weak getting weaker, now Telly watchers, the strong! But we will fight along! For those with ears to hear and eyes to see! The Geoengineering Insanity! The DNA modifying injections of Chemistry! 60 GHz mm Microwave Technology! Lock Downs, creating Poverty! Future travel with vaxxine passports and ID2020! Oh woe is me! We are for nature, creation and Ecology, to look after all lifeforms, on this planet from Whale to Bee! And here we are, both now in the UK! Are we not so Lucky? Where can we escape to? There is no PLANet B! We are here for a reason, so let it be!

Liberty Away!

So,

The virus PLANNEDemic

Has spread all over,

Almost every country,

The whole world over!

How can this be?

Pre Planned,

Obviously!

With control measures

In place,

To keep you,

In your place!

Witn restrictions,

On how many,

Can see your face!

Twelve weeks now

In Lock Down,

Self imprisonment,

With no allowance

For protest,

Or for an evening,

To go out!

This must be

Some KILLER

Virus,

Without a doubt?

Death figures,

Being inflated,

Main Stream Media,

Spreading fear!

Everyone with frowns

On their faces,

Very little

Good cheer!

No income for

Three months,

Hunger knocking,

At many a door!

Many will die

From starvation,

Lots will get sick,

As lots don't see,

The Sun

Too much,

Anymore!

Vitamin D depletion

Lowers the immune system,

Makes it weak

And almost every day,

Above your heads

They spray!

Nano particles of

Aluminium, Barium

And Strontium,

Which,

Once inhaled

Into your body,

Will not,

Go away!

Why is Dementia

And Altzheimers

Now the number one,

Killer of women in the UK?

DISease created

By an accumulation,

Of Aluminium

In the brain!

Which now,

On many thousands,

Or millions of families?

Is creating real strain!

"But it is the virus,

That they die

WITH not "FROM?"

We hear

Again and again!

Strange days

That we live in now,

That's for sure!

With Bill (God) Gates

Like a knight

In shining armour!

Coming up with a

Mandatory vaxxine,

Which has

Much more stuff in it,

Than just the supposed,

Virus cure!

He will make himself

A couple of

Hundred billion dollars,

Which will make him,

Happy in his head!

While humanity,

Will be either,

Dying. Sick,

Sterile,

Or dead?

The population

From sixty five million

To fifteen million in the UK,

In five years,

Deagel.com say!

Will you,

Be one of the

50 million,

That are

Going away?

Lets hope not,

Watch points,

Dont let them steal,

Our

Freedom

And

Liberty

Away!

Manifest!

MANIFEST

When seeking inspiration
For something new,
One has to go inside
To find out what to do,
For the inspiration
Is from the spirit
Who inspires
And guides
You through!

When dreaming of the future,
Of things you would like to be,
Your thoughts amass,
Then fly out,
Into universal energy!
Time ticks by whether
At work or at rest,
Until your dream
Becomes.....
Manifest!

Photo taken at my old home, The Irie Eyrie in South Africa.

More!

Interesting times that we live in but not funny!

It would seem,

As if,

A plan

Is underway!

At least,

It looks,

That way!

Bill Gates,

Recently

Announced,

That,

A

Pandemic,

Is on the way!

It could kill,

Millions of people,

He did say!

And his

Pirbright institute,

Funded lab,

Has a patent

For

Coronavirus,

Today!

So,

Then they

Hold a

Global,

Pandemic

Exercise!

Trying to

Make a

Future plan!

Then

Lo and behold,

The Coronavirus,

Is released,

In China,

In Wuhan!

Quite

Coincidentally,

Obviously!

With this city

And many

Others,

In complete

Lockdown mode,

With no Internet,

Or

Communications

But,

They do have,

The newly

Turned on

Internet of things,

Abbreviated as,

IOT!

With the

Facilitator

System,

Known as

Five Gee!

They have

No choice!

They have

No voice!

Locked in

Their homes,

While,

In the shadows,

No doubt,

The

Depopulation

Supporters,

Rejoice!

People taken

Against their will,

Violently!

To separation

Or

Concentration

Camps?

Not so

Discreetly!

Is this the

Future?

For

The rest,

Of

Humanity?

Funnily enough,

The symptoms

Between the two,

Are very alike!

A cough,

Fever,

Respiratory

Problems,

Headache!

And such

The like!

So,

Now,

The virus spreads,

By people,

On

Planes, boats

And other means!

Now,

Lo and behold!

We will have

Mandatory,

Untested,

Compulsory

Vaxxines!

Remember this,

While with

Your honey!

Out of this,

Some people,

Are going

To make,

A shitload

Of money!

Now,

Come new laws,

Introduced

Quietly,

In the UK!

Which say,

They,

(They)

Make come

And take

You away!

Twenty four hours

Initially,

Then increasing

To a fortnight,

Where in many

Different

Places,

Will

They,

Take you

To stay!

You know what is

Very handy,

When people die,

Of the

Supposed virus,

There is no

Autopsy!

It could be,

Coronavirus?

Then again,

It could be

Five Gee?

Now FEMA

Doing emergency drills,

For incarcerating

Many people

Against their wills!

They plan to take

People away,

From their homes,

Workplaces,

Airports,

Or railway stations?

Then lock you up

And give you,

Mandatory

Vaxxinations!

News channels

And the media,

Spreading fear,

And lies!

As we all live

Under poisonous,

Nano particulated

And Ionised,

Heavily

Geoengineered,

Skies!

In the old days

We used to

Call the shots!

But the times

They are

A changing!

With sweeping

New laws

And powers to do

With

Depopulation!

The writing,

Is on the wall,

As Sangomas

Throw the bones!

Their intentions

Are carved

In stone,

In the Georgia

Guide stones!

Evil,

At its core!

We don't want it,

Anymore!

Dear God,

Universal Spirit,

Creator,

Help and guide us,

For what lays

In

Store!

And show us,

How to bring,

Natures

Balance,

To

The earth,

Once

More!

5G

CORONAVIRUS

FEMA TO HOLD MASS CASUALTY DRILL

CORONAVIRUS NEWS

Educating Liberals
@Education4Libs

The Coronavirus:

-Outbreak found 20 miles from lab
that was CREATING it
-Gates predicted this virus could kill
65M people if released to the public
-Gates owns a patent for the vaccine
-Videos from Wuhan look like scenes
out of a horror movie

Bio-weapon? 🤔
You be the judge.

Not See!

This is so close

To the truth

In Scotland

Unfortunately,

As a lot

Of people

There,

Just

Do

Not

See!

Of Humanity!

Leslie Miller, I think the virus is a Smokescreen, for the mandatory vaxxine, Against a flu variant, that doesn't even kill that many, is what is crazy! Know what I mean? The NWO is on the way! Do we not already sit in our own home cells? No freedom to roam, or place open, to play? Everything is closed. Gyms, stadiums, theatres, bars and restaurants all boarded up, fronts in dismay! While above your head, in the skies they spray, almost every day! The even crazier part is that the sprays, they dont see, as being an actual threat, to Humanity! With Bill (God) Gates in the middle, of a web, of Iniquity! New Draconian rules, with accompanying fines, Geoengineering sprays put in place, to block the Sun,when it shines! Depriving us all of Vitamin D! Lowering our immune systems function, bad health cases we already see! Soon, we will have our One Year Anniversary! Of Lock Down! But we wont be able, to hold a Party! As the whole world is being affected, deliberate crashing, of the Global Economy! No longer free! Mask wearing being imposed, which is not healthy! Soon it will be ID2020! The Great RESET and Digital money! Social credit score, facial recognition, The IOT and many more! Changed days we live in now, heavily invested in controlled TV, spreading the common story, to the global masses, who also take their instructions and new rules from it also, with the new SMART TV! Me watching you and you watching me! Is what their slogan should be! Just think! Twelve months ago, we were free! Look at where we are now and surely, you can see, with the loss, of our employment! Hope's and dreams, almost instantly! Many choosing Suicide, not seeing any way to break free! People jumping off bridges, into rivers frequently! To escape, from the Globally imposed Stranglehold, on Humanity! All pre planned in Event 201! Less than two months, before the emergence and Grand Entry! In Wuhan, China, of a new flu strain, known as C_V_D! Since then, we have been under permanent, Self IMPRISONMENT with Tiers changing, the Severity! Some people are awake, to the SCAMMEDemic and meet, weekly! Sometimes getting hassled and arrested, by the ones that work, for the Authority! As thinkers, they are free! Get tagged, with the label of, Theorists in CONSPIRACY! To blow smoke in the eyes, of the Majority! But they will not be silenced, because they can see and are acting on behalf, of the future, of their family! Let us hope, that these numbers grow, for the sake, of Humanity!

One!

The
White Sun
Rises for
Another day!
It used to be
Yellow!
Do you
Remember that?
From days
Gone by,
Before they,
Started to
Spray?
Take a look
At your
Children's
Colouring book,
In the days
Of innocent fun!
When they
Coloured
In the
Sun,
It was
Always,
A
Yellow,
One!

Our Skies!

"The defence of

These islands,

Is the most

Important thing!"

Regarding Brexit

I heard,

Then thought,

"Is this the truth

Or lies?"

For if it were

The truth,

Then they

Wouldn't allow,

Anonymous planes

To poison

Our skies!

Flying every day,

Long white trails,

Criss crossing,

Then soon after,

They spread,

The Sun,

Goes away!

All of us breathing in

These Nano particles,

Not of our choice,

Or if we please?

After enough,

Then sure enough,

Along comes Dementia,

Or Alzheimer's disease?

Some nationalists

In Scotland,

See the

Sky Saltire,

As a sign!

Of Imminent,

Independence,

An Omen!

Aye, well fine!

So why do,

The Air Force,

And government,

Allow this

Obvious crime?

Because of

Approval of

Geoengineering,

Already for

Some time!

So,

To get back

To the

Original statement,

Does it sound,

Like truth or lies?

If it was true,

They wouldn't

Condone,

The spraying

Of our

Skies!

Party!

JiLof Aotearoa I just found videos that I took 12 months ago in an ancient bar in Glasgow called The Scotia first opened in 1793! Lots of people in there and lots playing! Great times, seems so long ago now! Since we lost our freedom, we had no choice, there was little that we could do! They have shut the world down and ruined the Global economy too! Because of the flu? You have a 99% chance of recovery if you get it, know what I mean? But now we have a crazy scene, because now we are being, coerced into taking one or more Vaxxine? For an overhyped, exaggerated, fear focused, statistically! Giving new rules and regulations daily! Keeping everyone programmed to what they watch on every TV! Clamping down on the Human population, Globally! Freedoms gone, already! And Liberty! Both are Already History! They have further plans you see! With our introduction to the world of 60GHz mm Microwave Technology and the IOT! Both moving on rapidly, while everyones attention is on the virus, so any symptoms from any one, in any way, gets listed in the statistics the same as deaths, since before last May! Wasn't meaning to write a poem, but it just turned out that way!
It started with the live music in the Scotia a year ago!
Will it ever go back to that? I do not know? But know that we are all living in our own home cell, our freedom gone! Life nowadays is not fun! No opportunity, businesses turning to rust! Going to Hell! Churches closed, no Bagpipe playing, singing, dancing, hugging, we are allowed nothing! Why? All done because of fear! Orchestrated, pre planned, all the continents it has spanned! In South Africa.They are wearing masks and social distancing too and all because of the same flu! For them, it must be a bummer because they have all this extra crap in their lives, in the middle of an African Summer! Do you see the Irony? With Bill (God) Gates involved from A to Z, donations to the Patent holder, holding Event 201, now we see him on TV! Telling us, what will be and how the future He! Does see! With vaxxines, for the whole worlds population, becoming Mandatory! To go on yearly! For Eternity! Everyone having ID 2020! Becoming part of the Matrix unknowingly! With millions kept quiet on Universal credit or Furlough money? Will this be continuing at its present rate, Permanently? What if it changes, what then? Not funny! Got many by the balls, Already! As a dependant on the state, they seal your fate! These changes are everywhere, they know no border! This beleive it or not is our free introduction to The New World Order! Moving behind the scenes, controlling and Orchestrating the Scenes! Agenda 2021 and 30 implementing! Doing everything for your Health and Safety! But tying you down, Ultimately! Which is where we are now, unfortunately! It is a very strange world now, that much, can be seen! With the latest virus like a Trojan horse or Massive Smokescreen? Where now is Democracy? With no canvassing allowed by any other Party?

Philanthropy?

Rob Preston:

Can't see it but he's posted in Anti

David Nicoll:

Oh, wonder why, a good example of Geoengineering there, wrote this poem in reply to him.

The link works for me!

The

Thought

Police,

(Fact

Checkers)

Maybe?

As

Bill,

Their boss,

Who funds

This shit,

Would

Not

Want,

The

People,

To

See!

The

Fruits,

Of

His,

Funding,

Of,

Geoengineering

And

Mix

It,

With

His

Philanthropy?

Poisonous spray!

Been travelling today,

In both Glasgow

And Edinburgh,

A common

Denominator,

Which I would

Like to say!

In both the skies

Their were,

Unnoticed,

Overhead,

Poisonous,

Spray!

Regret!

I call them

Long white streaks

In the sky!

As the word Chemtrails

Is looked on as a Conspiracy,

Even though these

Sun blocking,

Spreading streaks,

Criss cross our skies,

For those with eyes to see!

Some leaving almost

Unnatural colours in

Sunrise and Sunset,

Have seen videos of

The sprays being

Switched on and off,

So it's not caused

By wing tip vortices,

When the

Atmosphere is wet!

It is an assault on

Humanity and

All living life forms

On this

Glorious planet!

Much to my

Regret!

10

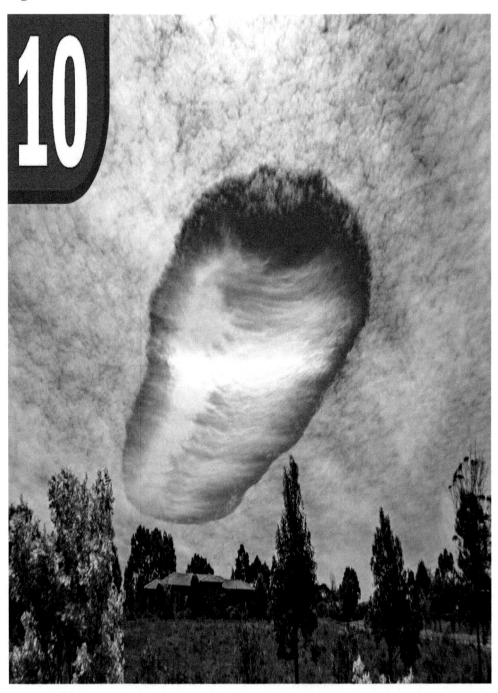

Save!

All life on this beautiful planet

That we call home,

Has come from one source!

If it were not for the Sun,

We would be an

Uninhabitable rock

With no life,

The Sun is our sole

Energy source!

The growth in all plants

Via photosynthesis!

Would not exist,

It would be cold and barren,

Its heat and radiance,

We would miss!

There would be no oil!

There would be no coal!

There would be no food!

There would be no sunshine!

It would be eternal darkness,

Not good for the Soul!

There would be

No birds, insects or animals!

There would be no trees!

There would be no food!

There would be frigid seas!

Now,

Because of the actions of man,

Some have decided to

Make a plan!

Due to the byproducts,

Of industry!

And experimental spraying,

We have

Holes in the ozone layer,

Which the naked eye,

Cannot see!

But we know that it is there,

Letting in harmful waves,

Skin cancer creating,

Rays of UVB!

So,

Surreptitiously and secretly,

We are being

Sprayed from above,

With coal fly ash

And many other things,

Which will lead many to

Death, sickness

And Insanity!

Although not that many

People this do see!

Although these long white

Streaks in the sky

Are there,

Plain as day

For all to see!

They say there is global warming

Which is really not fun

So,

Some Harvard University academics,

And the global ruling elite,

Have decided in their wisdom,

A way to sort this out,

Is to block the Sun!

This is happening everywhere,

From the ground and satellite

We see it all over,

From Australia, China,

Africa, America,

Europe and even

The white cliffs of Dover!

It is causing death,

It is causing Dis-Ease!

With the majority

Of Humanity,

Not being able to see,

The wood from the trees!

In a very short space

Of Universal time,

We have taken this

Pristine blue jewel,

With its natural balance,

Of nature in harmony!

To almost a point

Of no return,

Although this fact

Not many see!

So many problems and situations,

On the planet today!

From deforestation,

Species extinction,

Plastic pollution,

Forced vaccinations

And now Five Gee!

What will our future be?

What an absolute

Cock up we have made.

Of our custody!

Of the only habitable planet

That we know of,

Or can see!

Nature will strike back!

Of that you can be sure!

It does not sit on the fence,

For every action,

There is an equal and opposite

Reaction,

Although not that many

Can see this sense!

The curse of Homo Sapiens,

On whatever

He does feed!

Was his invention

Of a thing called Money,

And a feeling

Known as Greed!

But what good is all your money?

If this planet

We cannot save!

You cannot

And will not,

Take any of your money

To your grave!

Dear God and Universal Spirit!

Guide and help us,

So that,

Our Mother Earth

And all her Lifeforms,

We can Save!

Silver Grey!

As
Expected
After a
Heavy
Spray day!
The Sun,
Is well
And truly,
Hidden
Away!
Behind
Unnatural,
Clouds,
Of
Silver Grey!

Spraying?

All the

People saw,

Was four,

Long

White

Spreading,

Streaks,

In the sky!

Sprayed from

Very fast planes,

Streaking over our

Scottish sky,

Ever so high!

Photos appearing

On Facebook,

What can

They be?

Like loosly

Strung

Strings,

On a

Ukelele!

Then

The next day

"American jets,

Carried out,

Chemical

Warfare

Practice

Over

Edinburgh!"

In

Edinburgh

Live,

We do see!

An excercise,

Carried out,

By the

Military!

So that

Explains it,

Satisfying,

Our curiosity!

Only one question,

Remains to be

Answered,

Although,

No one,

Is saying!

Could you

Please

Tell us,

"What,

Were

You

Spraying?"

Stealing Our Sunshine!

Sun Away!

Saw a strange

Shadow in the sky

In the clouds

Above

George Square

In Glasgow,

Last Saturday!

What is it?

Well,

Who knows?

No one

Even

Noticed it,

Difficult

To say!

Could it be

That above,

There

Was an

Ariel

Spray?

Casting

Its

Shadow,

On the

Clouds

Below,

Fulfilling

Its

Purpose,

To

Block,

The

Sun,

Away!

The Only Way!

Two new

Phenomenon,

Which

Before,

Were

A

Rarity!

But now,

Much more,

Of both,

Do we see!

All over

The

World,

Funnily!

Birthed by

Planes,

Spreading

Aerosolised,

Metallic,

Nano

Particulates,

To

Reflect

The

Suns

Light back,

You see!

Add some

EMFs

Electro,

Magnetic,

Frequency!

Then the

Clouds line up,

Corrugatedly!

Before

Spreading

Easily,

Then no more,

Of the Sun,

Do you see!

Depriving you,

Of

Vitamin D!

And all

Life forms

Getting less,

Of the

Suns,

Energy!

Needed

For all

Natural,

Organic

Growth,

From

Plants,

To

Tree!

This

Spray

Is

Part of,

Our

Introduction,

Into the IOT*

As we breathe

These

Particulates in,

Very easily,

They then

Get absorbed,

Into your

Body,

Permanently!

With

Aluminium

Being

Especially

Reactive,

To

60 GHz mm

Microwave

Technology!

Which has,

Been

Turned on,

Recently!

In every

British

City!

But still,

People

Dont see!

The link

Between

The

Sprays

And

Technology!

They are,

No longer free!

Living in

Home cells,

In

Detention!

Seemingly,

Permanently!

Taking

Instructions,

From

Politicians,

Due to a

PLANNEDemic

Emergency!

Giving them

Powers,

To bend

Many rules,

Conveniently!

Issuing their

Message of

Fear and woe,

Statistically,

Daily!

Tying down,

The

Global

Populations,

Easily!

All

Coordinated

Secretly!

Acting as one,

All in the name,

Of our,

Health and Safety!

It started with

The flu,

"Stay at home

For three

Weeks to flatten

The curve!"

There was

Nothing,

That we,

Could do!

Now

One Year

Later,

We still sit,

Day after day,

While over our heads,

Treating us like bugs,

They spray!

Geoengineering

It is called,

Funded by our Bill,

For manys a day!

What of

The future?

Please

Tell people,

To wake

Them up,

As

It

Is,

The

Only way!

*=Internet Of Things

The Smokecreen!

The

Deceit

Being

Forced,

On the

Worlds

Population

Today!

Is absolute

Insanity!

To say

Otherwise,

Would be,

A

Miscarraige

Of

Justice,

To put it,

Another way!

Forcing people

To wear masks,

Decreasing,

The amount

Of

Oxygen,

Reaching

Your lungs,

Will,

On

Earth,

Shorten,

Your

Stay!

But,

"The

World

Is

Overpopulated!"

They,

The

Powers

That be,

Say!

So now,

A

Manfufactured,

Patented

Virus,

Has been

Released,

To

Global

Dismay!

All over

The planet,

New

Rules

And

Regulations,

Have been

Put,

Into

Force

Today!

Creating

Rebreathing,

Exhaled,

Carbon Dioxide,

From behind

Face masks,

Which restrict,

The in out

Natural flow,

Of your,

Throats,

Airway!

Creating

A

Division,

In

Humanity!

Between,

The

Sceptical,

Non beleivers

And those

That read,

The MSM

And watch

Daily,

TV!

Nowadays

You cannot

Believe

Anything,

That you

Hear,

Or

See?

Instigated

By an

Overhyped,

Flu variant,

Which is

Manipulated,

Statistically!

To keep

FEAR,

In the

Minds

And

Hearts,

Of all

Who see!

To follow,

The official

Narrative,

Unquestioningly!

A mass

Thinning,

Of the

Human

Herd,

Secretly,

And

Surrepticiously!

Helped along,

By the effects

Of

60GHz mm

Microwave,

Technology!

Which was

Installed,

Rapidly

And

Globally!

In the

Lock Down

Period,

Since last

March,

Discreetly!

By men in

White vans,

Operating,

Under

Vows,

Of

Secrecy!

And the

Cloak

Of

Darkness,

So as,

Not to

Be seen,

By the

Majority!

Who

Sit at

Home,

Under

Self

Imprisonment

And

House arrest,

Unknowingly!

Scared,

Of the new

Virus,

As anyone

Who dies,

From

Anything!

Gets listed

As

"WITH,

C_V_D!"

Why they

Worry

So much,

I do

Not know?

Because,

Even if you,

Were,

To catch it,

There is a

Ninety nine

Percent,

Recovery rate!

With a rapid

Recovery,

Not slow!

And no

Prescribed

Medicines,

To take

If you get it,

Just sit

At home

For fourteen

Days,

Where the

Time,

Will

Pass slow!

Outside of

Your house,

You are

Not allowed,

To go!

The flu,

Has been

Around

For millions

Of years!

Killing many

With

Compromised

Immune systems,

Leaving the

Bereaved

Left behind,

In

Tears!

With this latest

Man modified,

Variant,

There is

Also a

Ninety nine

Percent chance,

That you

Will not

Catch it!

"So,

What,

Is the

Problem?"

You might ask,

In good wit!

In truth

It is,

A

Trojan Horse!

To get to

The worlds

Population,

To decimate

Their numbers,

By putting

These new

Laws

Into force!

The likes

Of this,

Before,

Has never

Been seen!

The whole

PLANNEDemic

And

SCAMMEDemic,

Being a

Massive

Smokescreen!

To make

Everyone

So scared,

That they,

Will be

Queing up,

For the

As yet,

Uninvented

And

Untested

Vaxxine!

With

Bill (God) Gates,

Funding the

Seven main makers,

To make a

Twenty to one,

Return,

On his

Investments,

In them,

Which is,

Quite,

Obscene!

"Seven

Billion

People

Must

Have it!"

You see him

Saying,

On the

Screen!

Although

Have heard,

That

His three

Children,

Dont get

Vaccinated,

Strange that,

Know

What,

I mean?

Does he

Know,

Something

That we dont?

"They will

Not miss,

The second

Wave!"

He and his

Wife,

Smugly

Declared,

In an

Awful scene!

Whilst

Unkown,

To the

Majority,

A

New

World

Order

And

One

World

Government,

Gets

Organised,

Behind,

The

Smokescreen!

Their Lies!

He has a finger,

In so many pies!

From

GMOs,

Carbon capture,

Mass

Vaccinations

And

Geoengineering

Our skies!

Funding the

Fact Checkers,

On

Fakebook,

To make

Sure,

That we,

Do not,

See

Through,

Their

Lies!

The Telegraph

Tranquillity!

Right in front

Of everyone's eyes,

For the world to see,

Artifical clouds

Being affected

By

Electro

Magnetic

Frequency!

But how many

See that?

Not that many!

The latest

Panic induced

Global emergency,

Being about a virus

That you cannot

Even see!

Inflated figures

Being flounted

In the

Main Stream Media,

The Internet

And on TV!

To keep people

In a negative

State of fear,

You see!

People

Self imprisoned

Globally!

Not a nice

Sight to see!

Daily trails

In the skies,

Politicians lies!

With still,

No end in sight!

Track and Trace,

Wear a mask

On your face,

From any other person,

Stay two metres away!

These are only some

Of the laws today!

The next big thing,

Is the vaxxine,

Promised to the world,

By Mr Bill (God) Gates!

Who stands to make,

Hundreds of Billions

With some

Of his mates,

Every day,

We are

Breathing in,

Metalic

Nano particulates,

Of Aluminium,

Barium

And Strontium,

Which he also funds,

Through Geoengineering,

GMOs,

Investing in Monsanto,

Poisoning our food!

With pesticides

And herbicides,

For all organic life,

Not very good,

As for Vaxxines,

The seven main

Companies,

He is paying!

Or owning really?

Just another way

Of saying!

With plans to

Vaxxinate the planet,

That is everybody!

Then drastic reductions,

In the population

We would see,

With a slowing birth rate,

Due to vaxxine induced

Male and female,

Sterility!

There are many stories,

Of vaxxines gone wrong,

That is true,

Just take a look

At Vaxxed 1

And 2!

But what,

Can we do?

Say "No thanks?"

Will that do?

A wee point

To bear in mind,

That not many tell,

Is that the latest

Lab created virus,

Has been patented

And guess what?

He funds them

As well!

Has our freedom

Not now gone?

Should we

Kiss it

Goodbye?

"When are these,

New Draconian laws

Going to be

Rescinded?"

Some others will

Cry!

We are all now slaves,

To new trends,

Moves

And control

As far as I can see!

With ringing

In our ears

From 60GHz mm wave,

Technology!

Woe for the future,

Was this really meant?

Or being done,

By evil worshippers,

Who do it all,

Without consent!

But are doing it,

To usher in

A New

World

Government!

With people now

On their knees,

Fearing and feeling,

DIS ease!

Economies crashing,

Dreams dashing,

Red lights flashing!

With Vaxxines

You have no liability,

To sue,

No matter

What you do!

Should there be any

Side effects,

That come through!

Rumour has it,

That it is to do

With sterility,

Also to inject

A chip known

As RFID!

Radio

Frequency

IDentification,

Interesting times

That we live in,

Greed,

Control,

Power,

Depopulation,

Weather control,

Shaping the clouds,

Creating the winds,

Creating and deciding,

Which way?

Multiple

Hurricanes should run!

I wish,

Good health for everyone,

Regardless of who,

You may be!

With so much

Shit going on

All around us,

The future,

Who is to see?

In the meantime.

May you live

With food,

Water,

Shelter

And in

Tranquillity!

Today!

 Scottish People's Forum   ⋯
Group post by David Nicoll · 16 h · 🖾

https://m.facebook.com/groups/247636572620986/permalink/742961199755185/

 SMAAPP -Scottish Musicians and Artistes Against the Poisoning of our Planet
Group post by David Nicoll · ⬤ Admin · 20 h · 🖾

In the park with balls and in the sand pit, they play, without any of them, thinking anything, unusual, about the overhead Spray! What is it, with people today? Copyright David Nicoll 13.03.2021 www.davidnicoll.co.uk **Photo by** Renee Polgar in **New York City.**

Us Out!

Oh Mother Earth,

When you put yourself

Into space today,

Looking down,

Would make you sigh!

"Where are all the people?"

You would cry!

"The buildings are there,

But no people?

Am I going out,

Of my head?

Or are all the people,

Inside getting no Vitamin D?

And either dying or dead?

Or is it a global curfew?

Brought on by

The controlling elite?

The ones,

That you don't meet,

On the street!

Who,

A one world government,

They would like to make

Their plans come true!

With little,

It seems

That you can do!

A new man made patented virus,

Was released,

Leading to global avail!

And everyone on the planet

Was told to self isolate,

And keep yourself

In your own home,

Or should I say?

Open jail?

Dirty deeds in the meantime,

Getting done in the

Dead of night!

Infrastructure being installed

Surreptitiously!

For beaming out

60 GHz mm microwave

Technology!

With everyone on Lock Down,

Not many will see!

Our humanities freedom,

Now controlled you see!

An interesting situation,

Without a doubt!

And everyone wandering

"When are

THEY,

Going to let,

Us,

Out?"

#We Do Not Consent!

When

I lived

In

Africa,

It's

Endangerd

Wildlife

And

Habitat,

Took a focus,

Of my attention!

And the

Many atrocities,

That happen

Against it,

But in the

World news,

Rarely gets

A mention!

Not a focus,

Or

Priority?

Of

World

Attention!

Rhinos

Who have

Been here

For

Millenia,

Becoming

Extinct,

Because of

The

Massive

Eastern,

Demand

For

Rhino horn!

Elephant's

For their

Tusks,

Pangolin's for

Meat and scales/,

Lion's for

Canned

Hunting,

And

Skeletons,

Leopards

For their

Skin's

Which are

Tribally

And

Religiously

Worn!

Used to be

A voice,

In the

Wilderness,

Spreading

Stories,

In

Rhythm,

Meter

And

Rhyme,

Often,

With

The

African,

Djembe

Drums,

Powerful,

Primitive,

And

Sublime!

Now,

My

Attention,

From that,

Has been

Taken

Away!

By the lack

Of

Global

Freedom,

That

Humanity,

On the

Whole

Planet,

Has been

Taken

Away!

And all

Supposedly,

To do!

With

The

Flu!

So

They

Say!

What are

Now known,

As

Lock Down

Measures,

Mask

Wearing,

Social

Distancing!

On

Friend's

And

Neighbour's

Snitching!

Watching the

Daily statistics,

Of ,

Death,

Hospitalisation's,

But mainly

Of

Cases!

While everyone,

Must now wear,

Unhealthy masks,

Of any

Description?

To cover,

Their

Beautiful,

Unique

Smiling,

Faces!

This on

Its own,

Will create,

Great

Despair!

For we need,

In our bodies,

20%

Of

Oxygen,

To breathe

In our

Air!

Any less

Than this!

And your

Body,

Will go

Amiss!

Rebreathing,

Carbon

Dioxide,

Is not

Healthy,

As

Unfortunately,

The

Continual,

Mask wearing,

Which is in

Many places

Mandatory,

Is not going,

To work out

For them,

So well,

In the

Long term,

As they

Will see,

As it is,

Only a

Matter

Of time!

You see!

Then

Another,

Case,

Of

The

Latest

Virus,

You

Will,

Be

Termed,

As

Statistically!

With the same

Medical issue,

Respiratory!

Or

Pleurisy?

Facial

Blotches,

And

Raw skin,

For all to see!

With no

Apparent

Other reason,

For them being

There you see?

While

The

Masks,

Are

Being

Put on,

Willingly!

See someone

Without one,

He is,

A

Black

Sheep!

The

Rest of,

The

Flock,

Can see!

But he does,

Breathe free!

Not taking,

False

Information,

So willingly!

As we,

All get

Driven,

To the gate

Of have

A wee jag,

Or two?

In your arm,

If you want

Ever again,

To be free?

With a

Digital

ID2020?

Newly

Introduced

60 GHz mm

Microwave

Technology!

At that

Frequency,

Spinning,

Oxygen

Atoms,

Frantically!

So they don't

Transfer,

Through the

Haemoglobin,

Into our blood,

So easily!

Leaving the

Brain and

Internal

Organs,

With an

Oxygen,

Deficiency!

The same,

Symptoms,

Once again,

You will see!

Also

Will be

Registered,

As being

"With"

C_V_D!

To become,

Part,

Of the

Second wave,

Tsunami!

That filled,

Bill and

His wife,

With such

Glee!

How did

The future,

He forsee?

People under

House arrest,

Limited options,

Fines or

Jail terms?

For the chosen,

Or unlucky ones?

Getting handed out

Frequently!

Facebook pages,

YouTube channels,

Twitter accounts,

Shut down,

Immediately!

Including mine,

Unfortunately,

They dont want

The truth

Getting out

You see!

An ongoing,

Reality!

Still many,

Of

Humanity,

Do not yet see?

That they are

In the process

Of losing,

All their

Human rights,

Freedom

And

Liberty!

But the

Resistance,

Is now growing!

Many people,

In many lands,

In their number

Are showing!

That what

Is going,

Around

And

On,

They are

Now

Knowing!

Had enough

Of the deceit,

The false

Manufactured

Situation

That affects

Everyone,

No livelehood's

Left,

Disgruntled,

With the

Situation,

In number,

They are

Now indeed,

Growing!

Awake

And

Aware!

For each other,

Our families,

Children

And

Grandchildren

We care!

Our

Economy

Crashed,

Businesses

And jobs

All gone!

Not allowed

To do

Anything,

That you

Could

Regard,

As

Fun,

No singing!

No dancing!

No guitar,

Or in

Scotland

Only,

No

Bagpipe,

Practicing

Or

Playing?

Very

Selective

Ban that,

If you know,

What

I am,

Saying?

Lot's of

Sports not

Allowed,

Fooball matches

Being played

In

Stadium's

With no

Crowd!

Can't find

A

Piper

To play

At

Rallies

In

Holyrood,

Today!

They have

Taken,

Our

National

Spirit

And

Pride away!

As well

The social circle,

Casual chatting,

Romancing,

Highland

Dancing!

Now it's

Mask wearing!

Social distancing!

Think that this,

Might have,

A

Satanic ring?

And

That a

Spiritual

Intersession

And

Intervention,

Could be

Called for,

To reverse

Everything?

That

They

Have been,

Enabling!

Our

Human rights,

And

Freedom's,

They are

Stripping!

The times,

That we

Live in now,

Are certainly,

Interesting!

Dark forces,

In the

Background,

Organising!

For world

Domination,

Which they,

Want to be

Controlling!

With

Five million,

Children,

Every year,

Going missing!

Satanic rituals,

Adrenachrome!

Parent's,

Left,

Greiving!

Crying

And

Hissing!

DUMBS

Deep

Underground

Military

Bases,

Constantly,

Tunneling!

Into

Vaxxine

Productions,

Hundreds

Of

Billions,

Of

Dollars

And

Pounds,

Governments

Funneling!

Our future

Is

Charted,

It was

Not

Heaven sent!

We were not

Asked about,

Any of these

Imposed

Conditions,

That we find

Ourselves

In at the

Moment!

And would

Like to say,

#We Do Not

Consent!

WE DO NOT CONSENT

What are these long white streaks in the sky?

Chorus:

What are these long white streaks in the sky?

Being spread by many planes way up high!

They are not contrails!

They spread all over the sky!

Geoengineering, solar radiation management

Playing God with nature, controlling the weather!

Being done by the UN, without asking anyone

Or even having a blether?

Spreading Nano particulates of Barium and Strontium,

Also lots of Aluminium!

Why would they do this? You ask with a frown!

Knowing that Agenda 21s purpose

Is to bring the world population down!

Chorus

Everyone can see them

Spreading all over the global skies!

To cut down on sunlight supposedly

Playing God in disguise!

Denying everything, doing it on the sly!

As all can see it that have an eye!

Apart from the majority!

Who neither care nor see!

That our fate is linked

To these airborne particles most definitely!

Chorus

We must all come together

To fight this insanity!

Join Anti Geoengineering groups

On Facebook most definitely!

If not then your future will be decided

By others who would cut your life short,

And seal your destiny!

Don't let them do this

As we were all born

And God willing will

Remain alive and free!

Chorus instrumental and end.

Your Face!

Ruby McCann:

I saw that along with the big massive chem trail streak. You have taught me all of this and now I study those clouds with a different intensiveness. I saw a post on your page with an Aussie woman who was pointing out all the square clouds. Wonder if the chem trails brought sssssshhhhhh (whispering corona)? Hopefully I won't get attacked for asking that question. And, it might be a silly questions but saw a guy who said that its possible that they might do this during the second wave. I am only repeating what he said, so not sure, just asking.

David Nicoll:

You never know eh? Truth is often stranger than fiction? Glad that you are observing your surroundings more now Ruby. that lady is very good, glad that she is doing it now. Did you see the one she did showing Scotland? We dont know what is coming next but I am sure that they will surprise us with something, thats for sure. Apart from The One World Government, the Internet Of Things, digital money, mandatory vaxxines, Track and Trace, GMOs, Flouride, 60GHz mm EMF waves, two metre social distancing and wear a mask on your face!

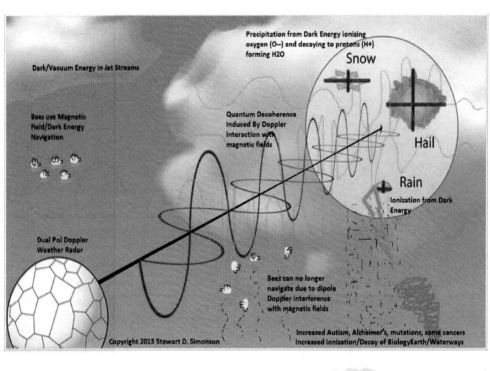

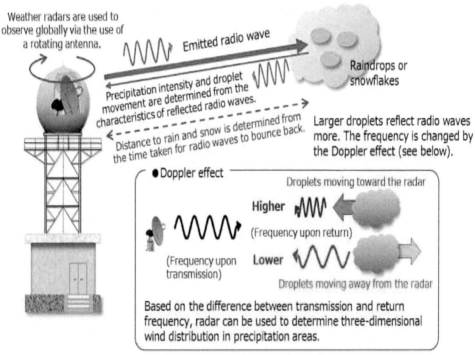

EMFs Electro Magnetic Frequency

The Way Clouds Used To Be!

New Cloud Formations as shown in The International Cloud Atlas!

Where did they come from all of a sudden?

No New Cloud Formations for 30 years and all of a sudden we have 11 new ones.

Ro

ll/Volutus

Asperitas

Wall cloud with a tail cloud

Kelvin-Helmholtz Wave Clouds

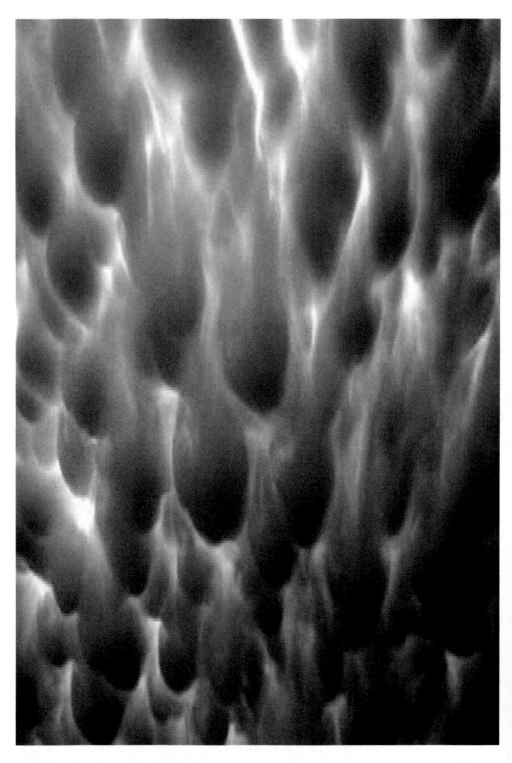

Mammatus clouds

Mammatus clouds

Mammatus clouds

Geekologie

Undulatus Asperatus

Asperitas

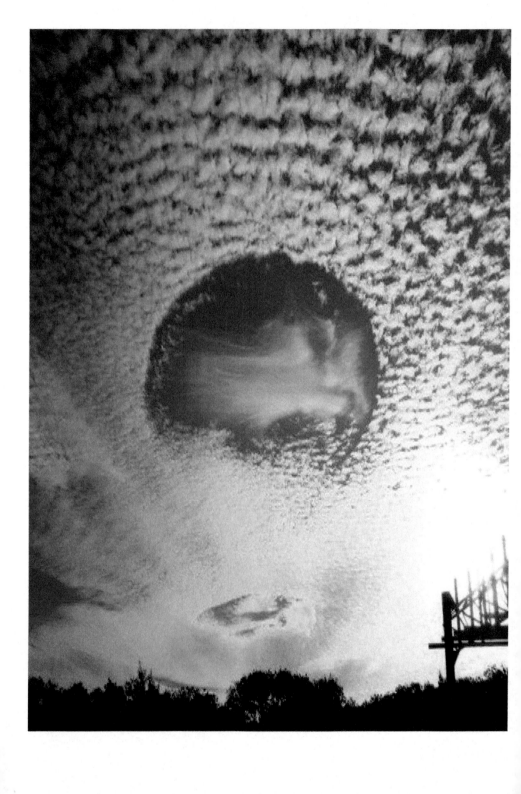

Homogenitus clouds

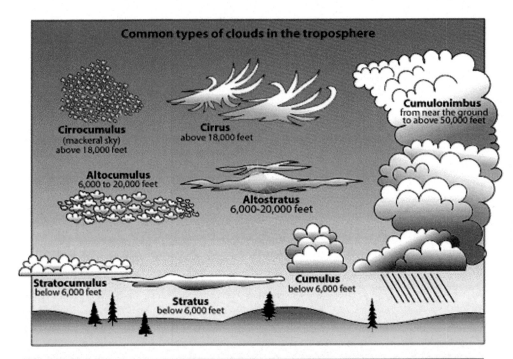

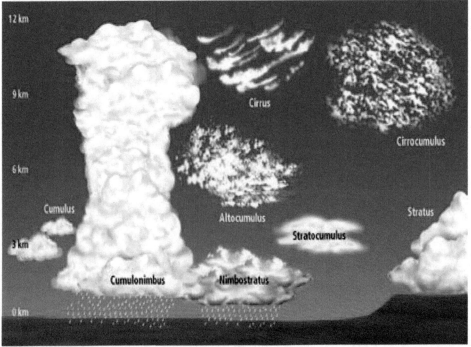

Common type of clouds

STANDARD CLOUD TYPE CHART

Cloud chart showing the different types of high, mid, and low-level clouds, as well as a number of other interesting cloud types and formations.

Geoengineering Photo Gallery!

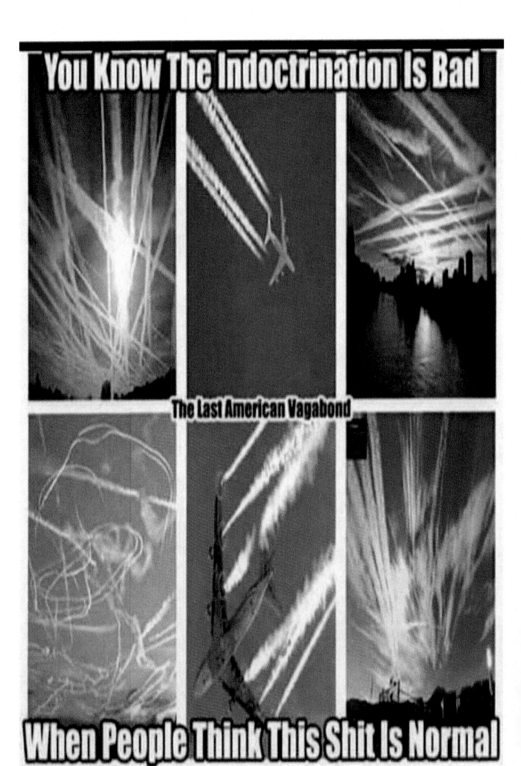

USA!

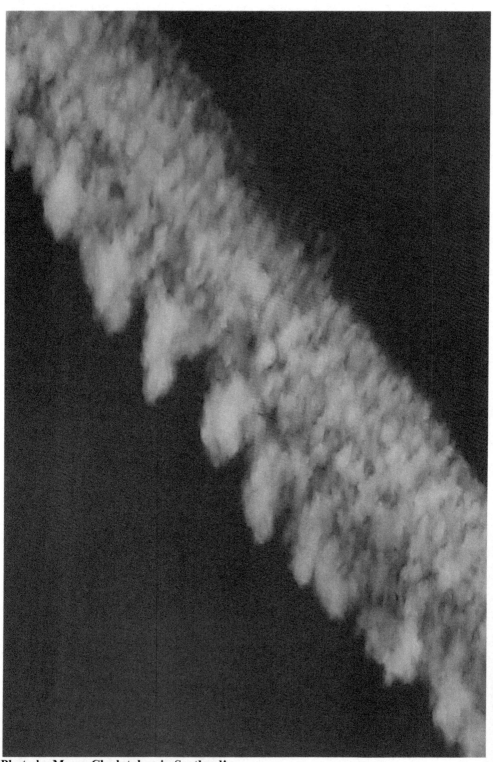

Photo by Momo Clark taken in Scotland!

Manchester, England!

Cape Town, South Africa!

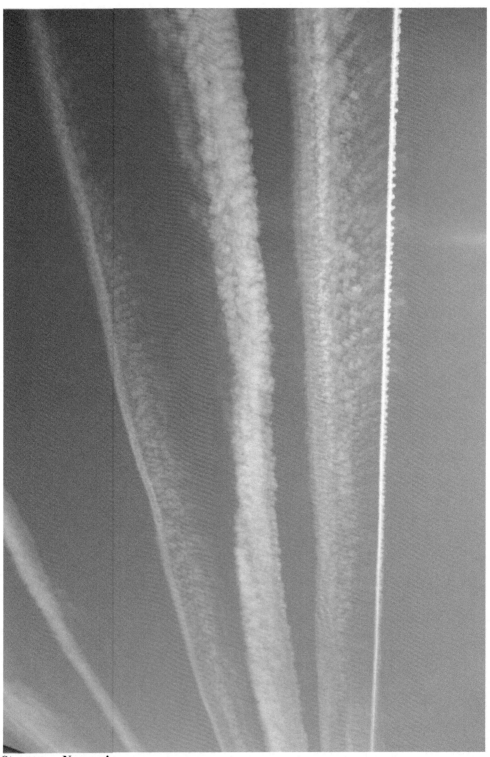

Stavanger, Norway!

The Alps!

Photo by Emory Eugene Mullen in California!

Mount Fuji, Japan.

Photo by Momo Clark in Glasgow, Scotland!

Kommetjie, South Africa!

Glasgow, Scotland!

If you enjoyed the book,

Please do a review!

On

Geoengineering pages,

Amazon,

Facebook,

Or any other

Platforms!

Thank you!

www.davidnicoll.co.uk

Printed in Great Britain
by Amazon

38629335R00136